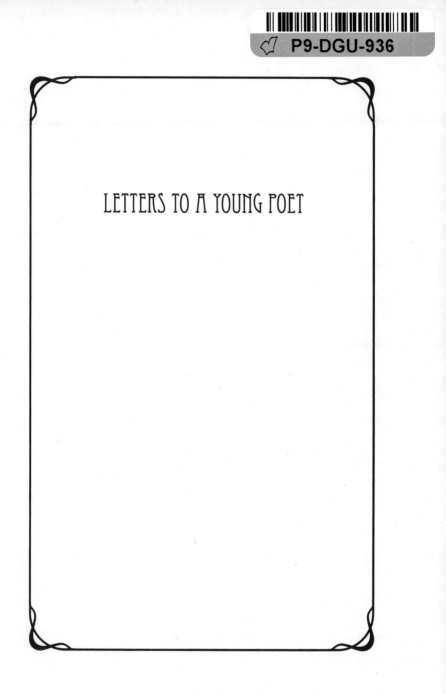

LETTERS TO A YOUNG POET

RAINER MARIA RILKE

In Translations by M. D. Herter Norton
Letters to a Young Poet
Sonnets to Orpheus
Wartime Letters to Rainer Maria Rilke
Translations from the Poetry of Rainer Maria Rilke
The Lay of the Love and Death of Cornet Christopher Rilke
The Notebooks of Malte Laurids Brigge
Stories of God

Translated by Jane Bannard Greene and M. D. Herter Norton
Letters of Rainer Maria Rilke. Volume One, 1892–1910
Letters of Rainer Maria Rilke. Volume Two, 1910–1926

Translated by David Young
Duino Elegies

In Various Translations
Rilke on Love and Other Difficulties. Translations and
Considerations of Rainer Maria Rilke
Compiled by John J. L. Mood

Translated by Edward Snow and Michael Winkler
Diaries of a Young Poet

RAINER MARIA RILKE
LETTERS TO A YOUNG POET

Translation by M. D. Herter Norton

Revised Edition

W. W. Norton & Company New York London

Reissued in Norton paperback 2004

ISBN 978-0-393-31039-9

Manufacturing by LSC, Harrisonburg

Book design by Blue Shoe Studio

Production manager; Amanda Morrison

W. W. Norton & Company, Inc.

500 Fifth Avenue, New York, N.Y. 10110

www.wwnorton.com

W. W. Norton & Company Ltd.

15 Carlisle Street, London W1D 3BS

Printed in the United States of America

38 39 40

CONTENTS

TRANSLATOR'S NOTE

How these letters came to be written is told by their recipient in his introduction, and to this there would be nothing to add were it not for the close of the eighth letter: "Do not believe that he who seeks to comfort you lives untroubled among the simple and quiet words that sometimes do you good. His life has much difficulty and sadness. . . . Were it otherwise he would never have been able to find those words." It is evident that a great artist, whatever the immediate conditions disturbing his own life, may be able to clarify for the benefit of another those fundamental truths the conviction of which lies too deep in his consciousness to be reached by external agitations. Though Rilke expresses himself with a wisdom and a kindness that seem to reflect the calm of self-possession, his spirit may have been speaking out of its own need rather than from the security of ends achieved, so that his words indeed reflect desire rather than fulfillment. In what sort this was the case becomes apparent on perusal of the several volumes of his correspondence. From these, for the most part, the accompanying chronicle of the years 1903–1908 has been prepared. It shows what Rilke was going through in his own relationship to life and work at the period in question (he turned twenty-eight in December, 1903). Perhaps such a record may in a measure explain, too, why sympathy was always so responsive an element of his nature. Certainly—despite low physical vitality that often reduced him to actual ill-health, despite lack of funds and homeless wandering in search of the right places and circumstances for his work, despite all the subjective fret and hindrance because of which some think to see in him a morbidly conditioned fantasy—the legend of the weary poet is dispelled, and in the end we find him always young, always constructive, the eminently positive philosopher of these letters.

New York, October, 1934

In revising the text for the present edition the translator is indebted to Herbert Steiner for many helpful criticisms and suggestions.

Washington, D.C., February, 1954

INTRODUCTION

It was in the late autumn of 1902—I was sitting under some ancient chestnuts in the park of the Military Academy in Wiener-Neustadt, reading. So deeply was I absorbed in my book, I scarcely noticed when the only civilian among our professors, the Academy's learned and kindly Parson Horaček, came to join me. He took the volume from my hand, contemplated the cover, and shook his head. "Poems of Rainer Maria Rilke?" he asked reflectively. He then turned the pages here and there, skimmed a couple of verses, gazed thoughtfully into the distance, and finally nodded. "So our pupil René Rilke has become a poet."

And I learned of the thin, pale boy, whom his parents had sent more than fifteen years ago to the Lower Military School at Sankt-Pölten so that he might later become an officer. Horaček had been chaplain to that institution at the time, and he still remembered his former student perfectly. He described him as a quiet, serious, highly endowed boy, who liked to keep to himself, patiently endured the compulsions of boarding-school life and after his fourth year moved on with the others into the Military College, which was situated at Mährisch-Weisskirchen. Here indeed it became apparent that his constitution could not stand the strain, for which reason his parents removed him from the school and let him continue his studies at home in Prague. How the course of his life had since shaped itself Horaček could not say.

After all this it is not hard to understand how I determined in that very hour to send my poetic attempts to Rainer Maria Rilke and to ask him for his opinion. Not yet twenty, and close on the threshold of a profession which I felt to be entirely contrary to my inclinations, I hoped to find understanding, if in any one, in the poet who had written *Mir zur Feier*. And without having intended to do so at all, I found myself writing a covering letter in which I unreservedly laid bare my heart as never before and never since to any second human being.

Many weeks passed before a reply came. The blue-sealed letter bore the postmark of Paris, weighed heavy in the hand, and showed on the envelope the same beautiful, clear, sure characters in which the text was set down from the first line to the last. With it began my regular correspondence with Rainer Maria Rilke which lasted until 1908 and then gradually petered out because life drove me off into those very regions from which the poet's warm, tender and touching concern had sought to keep me.

But that is not important. Only the ten letters are important that follow here, important for an understanding of the world in which Rainer Maria Rilke lived and worked, and important too for many growing and evolving spirits of today and tomorrow. And where a great and unique man speaks, small men should keep silence.

Franz Xaver Kappus
Berlin, June 1929

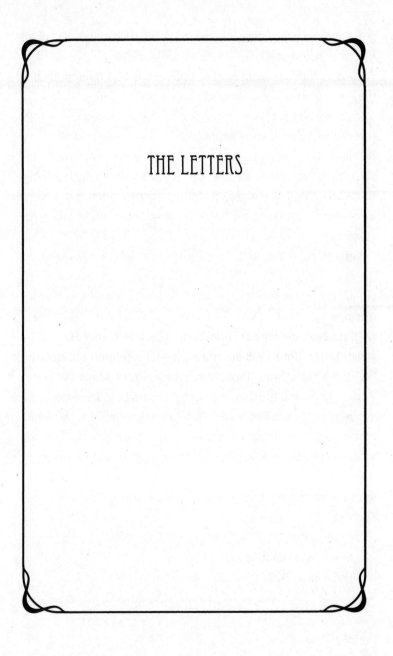

THE LETTERS

ONE

Paris,
February 17th, 1903

My dear sir,

Your letter only reached me a few days ago. I want to thank you for its great and kind confidence. I can hardly do more. I cannot go into the nature of your verses; for all critical intention is too far from me. With nothing can one approach a work of art so little as with critical words: they always come down to more or less happy misunderstandings. Things are not all so comprehensible and expressible as one would mostly have us believe; most events are inexpressible, taking place in a realm which no word has ever entered, and more inexpressible than all else are works of art, mysterious existences, the life of which, while ours passes away, endures.

After these prefatory remarks, let me only tell you further that your verses have no individual style, although they do show quiet and hidden beginnings of something personal. I feel this most clearly in the last poem, "My Soul." There something of your own wants to come through to word and melody. And in the lovely poem "To Leopardi" there does perhaps grow up a sort of kinship with that great solitary man. Nevertheless the poems are not yet anything on their own account, nothing independent, even the last and the one to Leopardi. Your kind letter, which accompanied them, does not fail to make clear to me various shortcomings which I felt in reading your verses without however being able specifically to name them.

You ask whether your verses are good. You ask me. You have asked others before. You send them to magazines. You compare them with other poems, and you are disturbed when certain editors reject your efforts. Now (since you have allowed me to advise you) I beg you to give up all that. You are looking outward, and that above all you should not do now. Nobody can counsel and help you, nobody. There is only one single way. Go into yourself. Search for the reason that bids you write; find out whether it is spreading out its roots in the deepest places of your heart, acknowledge to yourself whether you would have to die if it were denied you to write. This above all—ask yourself in the stillest hour of your night: *must* I write? Delve into yourself for a deep answer. And if this should be affirmative, if you may meet this earnest question with a strong and simple "I *must*," then build your life according to this necessity; your life even into its most indifferent and slightest hour must be a sign of this urge and a testimony to it. Then draw near to Nature. Then try, like some first human being, to say what you see and experience and love and lose. Do not write love-poems; avoid at first those forms that are too facile and commonplace: they are the most difficult, for it takes a great, fully matured power to give something of your own where good and even excellent traditions come to mind in quantity. Therefore save yourself from these general themes and seek those which your own everyday life offers you; describe your sorrows and desires, passing thoughts and the belief in some sort of beauty—describe all these with loving, quiet, humble sincerity, and use, to express yourself, the things in your environment, the images from your dreams, and the objects of your memory. If your daily life seems poor, do not blame it; blame yourself, tell yourself that you are not poet enough to call forth its riches; for to the creator there is no poverty and no poor indifferent place. And even if you were in some prison the walls of which let none of the sounds of the world come to your senses—would you not then still have your childhood, that precious, kingly possession, that treasure-house of memories? Turn your attention thither. Try to raise the submerged sensations of that ample past; your personality will grow more firm, your solitude will widen and will become a dusky dwelling past which the noise of others goes by far away.—And if out of this turning inward, out of this absorption into your own world *verses* come, then it will not occur to you to ask anyone whether they are good *verses*.. Nor will you try to interest magazines in your poems: for you will see in them your fond natural possession, a fragment and a voice of your life. A work of art is good if it has sprung from necessity. In this nature of its origin lies the judgment of it: there is no other. Therefore, my dear sir, I know no advice for you save this: to go into yourself and test the deeps in which your life takes rise; at its source you will find the answer to the question whether you *must* create. Accept it, just as it sounds, without inquiring into it. Perhaps it will turn out that you are called to be an artist. Then take that destiny upon yourself and bear it, its burden and its greatness, without ever asking what recompense might come from outside. For the creator must be a world for himself and find everything in himself and in Nature to whom he has attached himself.

But perhaps after this descent into yourself and into your inner solitude you will have to give up becoming a poet; (it is enough, as I have said, to feel that one could live without writing: then one must not attempt it at all). But even then this inward searching which I ask of you will not have been in vain. Your life will in any case find its own ways thence, and that they may be good, rich and wide I wish you more than I can say.

What more shall I say to you? Everything seems to me to have its just emphasis; and after all I do only want to advise you to keep growing quietly and seriously throughout your whole development; you cannot disturb it more rudely than by looking outward and expecting from outside replies to questions that only your inmost feeling in your most hushed hour can perhaps answer.

It was a pleasure to me to find in your letter the name of Professor Horaček; I keep for that lovable and learned man a great veneration and a gratitude that endures through the years. Will you, please, tell him how I feel; it is very good of him still to think of me, and I know how to appreciate it.

The verses which you kindly entrusted to me I am returning at the same time. And I thank you once more for your great and sincere confidence, of which I have tried, through this honest answer given to the best of my knowledge, to make myself a little worthier than, as a stranger, I really am.

Yours faithfully and with all sympathy:
Rainer Maria Rilke

TWO

Viareggio, near Pisa (Italy),
April 5th, 1903

You must forgive me, my dear sir, for only today gratefully remembering your letter of February 24th: I have been unwell all this time, not exactly ill, but oppressed by an influenza-like lassitude that has made me incapable of anything. And finally, as I simply did not get better, I came to this southerly sea, the beneficence of which has helped me once before. But I am not yet well, writing comes hard to me, and so you must take these few lines for more.

Of course you must know that every letter of yours will always give me pleasure, and only bear with the answer which will perhaps often leave you empty-handed; for at bottom, and just in the deepest and most important things, we are unutterably alone, and for one person to be able to advise or even help another, a lot must happen, a lot must go well, a whole constellation of things must come right in order once to succeed.

Today I wanted to tell you just two things more:

Irony: Do not let yourself be governed by it, especially not in uncreative moments. In creative moments try to make use of it as one more means of grasping life. Cleanly used, it too is clean, and one need not be ashamed of it; and if you feel you are getting too familiar with it, if you fear this growing intimacy with it, then turn to great and serious objects, before which it becomes small and helpless. Seek the depth of things: thither irony never descends— and when you come thus close to the edge of greatness, test out at the same time whether this ironic attitude springs from a necessity of your nature. For under the influence of serious things either it will fall from you (if it is something fortuitous), or else it will (if it really innately belongs to you) strengthen into a stern instrument and take its place in the series of tools with which you will have to shape your art.

And the second point about which I wanted to tell you today is this:

Of all my books just a few are indispensable to me, and two even are always among my things, wherever I am. They are about me here too: the Bible, and the books of the great Danish writer, Jens Peter Jacobsen. I wonder whether you know his works. You can easily get them, for some of them have come out in very good translation in Reclam's Universal Library. Get yourself the little volume of *Six Stories* of J. P. Jacobsen and his novel *Niels Lyhne*, and start on the first story in the former, called "Mogens. " A world will come over you, the happiness, the abundance, the incomprehensible immensity of a world. Live a while in these books, learn from them what seems to you worth learning, but above all love them. This love will be repaid you a thousand and a thousand times, and however your life may turn,—it will, I am certain of it, run through the fabric of your growth as one of the most important threads among all the threads of your experiences, disappointments and joys.

If I am to say from whom I have learned something about the nature of creative work, about its depth and everlastingness, there are but two names I can mention: that of Jacobsen, the great, great writer, and that of Auguste Rodin, the sculptor, who has not his equal among all artists living today.

And all success upon your ways!

Yours:
Rainer Maria Rilke

THREE

Viareggio, *near* Pisa (Italy),
April 23rd, 1903

You gave me much joy, my dear sir, with your Easter letter; for it said many good things about yourself, and the way you spoke of Jacobsen's great and beloved art showed me that I had not erred in guiding your life and its many questions to this source of plenty.

Now *Niels Lyhne* will open up before you, a book of glories and of the deeps; the oftener one reads it—there seems to be everything in it from life's very faintest fragrance to the full big taste of its heaviest fruits. There is nothing that does not seem to have been understood, grasped, experienced and recognized in the tremulous after-ring of memory; no experience has been too slight, and the least incident unfolds like a destiny, and fate itself is like a wonderful, wide web in which each thread is guided by an infinitely tender hand and laid alongside another and held and borne up by a hundred others. You will experience the great happiness of reading this book for the first time, and will go through its countless surprises as in a new dream. But I can tell you that later too one goes through these books again and again with the same astonishment and that they lose none of the wonderful power and surrender none of the fabulousness with which they overwhelm one at a first reading.

One just comes to relish them increasingly, to be always more grateful, and somehow better and simpler in one's contemplating, deeper in one's belief in life, and in living happier and bigger.

And later you must read the wonderful book of the destiny and desire of *Marie Grubbe* and Jacobsen's letters and pages from his diary and fragments and finally his poems, which (even if they are only fairly well translated) live in everlasting sound. (For this purpose I would advise you to buy when you have a chance the beautiful complete edition of Jacobsen's works which contains all these. It appeared in three volumes, well translated, brought out by Eugen Diederichs in Leipzig, and costs, I believe, only 5 or 6 marks a volume.)

In your opinion of "There should have been roses . . ." (that work of such incomparable delicacy and form) you are of course quite, quite unassailably right as against the writer of the introduction. And let me here promptly make a request: read as little as possible of aesthetic criticism—such things are either partisan views, petrified and grown senseless in their lifeless induration, or they are clever quibblings in which today one view wins and tomorrow the opposite. Works of art are of an infinite loneliness and with nothing so little to be reached as with criticism. Only love can grasp and hold and be just toward them. Consider *yourself* and your feeling right every time with regard to every such argumentation, discussion or introduction; if you are wrong after all, the natural growth of your inner life will lead you slowly and with time to other insights. Leave to your opinions their own quiet undisturbed development, which, like all progress, must come from deep within and cannot be pressed or hurried by anything. *Everything* is gestation and then bringing forth. To let each impression and each germ of a feeling come to completion wholly in itself, in the dark, in the inexpressible, the unconscious, beyond the reach of one's own intelligence, and await with deep humility and patience the birth-hour of a new clarity: that alone is living the artist's life: in understanding as in creating.

There is here no measuring with time, no year matters, and ten years are nothing. Being an artist means, not reckoning and counting, but ripening like the tree which does not force its sap and stands confident in the storms of spring without the fear that after them may come no summer. It does come. But it comes only to the patient, who are there as though eternity lay before them, so unconcernedly still and wide. I learn it daily, learn it with pain to which I am grateful: *patience* is everything!

Richard Dehmel: His books affect me (and, incidentally, so does the man whom I know casually) in such a manner that when I have found one of his beautiful pages I am always afraid of the next, which may upset everything again and turn what is attractive into something unworthy. You characterized him very well with the term: "living and writing in heat."— And in fact artistic experience lies so incredibly close to that of sex, to its pain and its ecstasy, that the two manifestations are indeed but different forms of one and the same yearning and delight. And if instead of heat one might say—sex, sex in the great, broad, clean sense, free of any insinuation of ecclesiastical error, then his art would be very grand and infinitely important. His poetic power is great, strong as a primitive instinct; it has its own unyielding rhythms in itself and breaks out of him as out of mountains.

But it seems that this power is not always honest and without pose. (But this again is one of the hardest tests of the creative individual: he must always remain unconscious, unsuspecting of his best virtues, if he would not rob them of their ingenuousness and untouchedness!) And then, where, as it rushes through his being, it comes to the sexual, it finds not quite so pure a man as it might require. Here is no thoroughly mature and clean sex world, but one that is not sufficiently *human*, that is only *male*, is heat, intoxication and restlessness, and laden with the old prejudices and arrogances with which man has disfigured and burdened love. Because he loves as man *only*, not as human being, for this reason there is in his sexual feeling something narrow, seeming wild, spiteful, time-bound, uneternal, that diminishes his art and makes it ambiguous and doubtful. It is *not* immaculate, it is marked by time and by passion, and little of it will survive and endure. (But most art is like that!) Nevertheless one may deeply rejoice in what there is of greatness in it, only one must not lose oneself in it and become an adherent of that Dehmelian world which is so unspeakably apprehensive, full of adultery and confusion, and so far from the real destinies that cause more suffering than these temporal afflictions but also give more opportunity for greatness and more courage for eternity.

Finally, as to my books, I would like best to send you all that might give you pleasure. But I am very poor, and my books, when once they have appeared, no longer belong to me. I cannot buy them myself—and, as I would so often like, give them to those who would be kind to them.

So I am writing you on a slip the titles (and publishers) of my most recent books (the latest, in all I believe I have published some 12 or 13) and must leave it to you, dear sir, to order some of them when occasion offers.

I like to think of my books as in your possession.

Farewell.

Yours:
Rainer Maria Rilke

FOUR

Worpswede, near Bremen,
July 16*th,* 1903

Some ten days ago I left Paris, quite ill and tired, and jour-
neyed into a great northerly plain whose breadth and stillness
and sky are to make me well again. But I came into a long spell of
rain that today for the first time shows signs of clearing a little
over the restlessly wind-blown land; and I am using this first
moment of brightness to greet you, dear sir.

Very dear Mr. Kappus: I have left a letter from you long unan-
swered, not that I had forgotten it—on the contrary: it was of the
sort that one reads again, when one finds them among one's cor-
respondence, and I recognized you in it as though you had been
close at hand. It was the letter of May 2nd, and you surely remem-
ber it. When I read it, as now, in the great quiet of these dis-
tances, I am touched by your beautiful concern about life, more
even than I had felt it in Paris, where everything resounds and
dies away differently because of the too great noise that makes
things vibrate. Here, where an immense country lies about me,
over which the winds pass coming from the seas, here I feel that
no human being anywhere can answer for you those questions
and feelings that deep within them have a life of their own; for
even the best err in words when they are meant to mean most
delicate and almost inexpressible things. But I believe neverthe-

less that you will not have to remain without a solution if you will hold to objects that are similar to those from which my eyes now draw refreshment. If you will cling to Nature, to the simple in Nature, to the little things that hardly anyone sees, and that can so unexpectedly become big and beyond measuring; if you have this love of inconsiderable things and seek quite simply, as one who serves, to win the confidence of what seems poor: then everything will become easier, more coherent and somehow more conciliatory for you, not in your intellect, perhaps, which lags marveling behind, but in your inmost consciousness, waking and cognizance. You are so young, so before all beginning, and I want to beg you, as much as I can, dear sir, to be patient toward all that is unsolved in your heart and to try to love the *questions themselves* like locked rooms and like books that are written in a very foreign tongue. Do not now seek the answers, which cannot be given you because you would not be able to live them. And the point is, to live everything. *Live* the questions now. Perhaps you will then gradually, without noticing it, live along some distant day into the answer. Perhaps you do carry within yourself the possibility of shaping and forming as a particularly happy and pure way of living; train yourself to it—but take whatever comes with great trust, and if only it comes out of your own will, out of some need of your inmost being, take it upon yourself and hate nothing. Sex is difficult; yes. But they are difficult things with which we have been charged; almost everything serious is difficult, and everything is serious. If you only recognize this and manage, out of yourself, out of your *own* nature and ways, out of your *own* experience and childhood and strength to achieve a relation to sex wholly your own (*not* influenced by convention and custom), then you need no longer be afraid of losing yourself and becoming unworthy of your best possession.

Physical pleasure is a sensual experience no different from pure seeing or the pure sensation with which a fine fruit fills the tongue; it is a great unending experience, which is given us, a knowing of the world, the fullness and the glory of all knowing. And not our acceptance of it is bad; the bad thing is that most people misuse and squander this experience and apply it as a stimulant at the tired spots of their lives and as distraction instead of a rallying toward exalted moments. Men have made even eating into something else: want on the one hand, superfluity upon the other, have dimmed the distinctness of this need, and all the deep, simple necessities in which life renews itself have become similarly dulled. But the individual can clarify them for himself and live them clearly (and if not the individual, who is too dependent, then at least the solitary man). He can remember that all beauty in animals and plants is a quiet enduring form of love and longing, and he can see animals, as he sees plants, patiently and willingly uniting and increasing and growing, not out of physical delight, not out of physical suffering, but bowing to necessities that are greater than pleasure and pain and more powerful than will and withstanding. O that man might take this secret, of which the world is full even to its littlest things, more humbly to himself and bear it, endure it, more seriously and feel how terribly difficult it is, instead of taking it lightly. That he might be more reverent toward his fruitfulness, which is but *one*, whether it seems mental or physical; for intellectual creation too springs from the physical, is of one nature with it and only like a gentler, more ecstatic and more everlasting repetition of physical delight. "The thought of being creator, of procreating, of making" is nothing without its continuous great confirmation and realization in the world, nothing without the thousandfold concordance from things and animals—and enjoyment of it is so indescribably beautiful and rich only because it is full of inherited memories of the begetting and the bearing of millions. In one creative thought a thousand forgotten nights of love revive, filling it with sublimity and exaltation. And those who come together in the night and are entwined in rocking delight do an earnest work and gather sweetnesses, gather depth and strength for the song of some coming poet, who will arise to speak of ecstasies beyond telling. And they call up the future; and though they err and embrace blindly, the future comes all the same, a new human being rises up, and on the ground of that chance which here seems consummated, awakes the law by which a resistant vigorous seed forces its way through to the egg-cell that moves open toward it. Do not be bewildered by the surfaces; in the depths all becomes law. And those who live the secret wrong and badly (and they are very many), lose it only for themselves and still hand it on, like a sealed letter, without knowing it. And do not be confused by the multiplicity of names and the complexity of cases. Perhaps over all there is a great motherhood, as common longing. The beauty of the virgin, a being that (as you so beautifully say) "has not yet achieved anything," is motherhood that begins to sense itself and to prepare, anxious and yearning. And the mother's beauty is ministering motherhood, and in the old woman there is a great remembering. And even in the man there is motherhood, it seems to me, physical and spiritual; his procreating is also a kind of giving birth, and giving birth it is when he creates out of inmost fullness. And perhaps the sexes are more related than we think, and the great renewal of the world will perhaps consist in this, that man and maid, freed of all false feelings and reluctances, will seek each other not as opposites, but as brother and sister, as neighbors, and will come together *as human beings*, in order simply, seriously and patiently to bear in common the difficult sex that has been laid upon them.

But everything that may some day be possible to many the solitary man can now prepare and build with his hands, that err less. Therefore, dear sir, love your solitude and bear with sweet-sounding lamentation the suffering it causes you. For those who are near you are far, you say, and that shows it is beginning to grow wide about you. And when what is near you is far, then your distance is already among the stars and very large; rejoice in your growth, in which you naturally can take no one with you, and be kind to those who remain behind, and be sure and calm before them and do not torment them with your doubts and do not frighten them with your confidence or joy, which they could not understand. Seek yourself some sort of simple and loyal community with them, which need not necessarily change as you yourself become different and again different; love in them life in an unfamiliar form and be considerate of aging people, who fear that being-alone in which you trust. Avoid contributing material to the drama that is always stretched taut between parents and children; it uses up much of the children's energy and consumes the love of their elders, which is effective and warming even if it does not comprehend. Ask no advice from them and count upon no understanding; but believe in a love that is being stored up for you like an inheritance and trust that in this love there is a strength and a blessing, out beyond which you do not have to step in order to go very far!

It is good that you are presently entering a profession that will make you independent and set you entirely on your own in every sense. Wait patiently to find out whether your inner life feels cramped by the form of this profession. I consider it very difficult and very exacting, as it is burdened with great conventions and scarcely leaves room for a personal conception of its problems. But your solitude will be a hold and home for you even amid very unfamiliar conditions and from there you will find all your ways. All my wishes are ready to accompany you, and my confidence is with you.

Yours:
Rainer Maria Rilke

FIVE

Rome,
October 29th, 1903

My dear sir,

I received your letter of August 29th in Florence, and not till now—two months later—am I telling you of it. Forgive this dilatoriness—but I do not like writing letters while traveling, because I need more for letter-writing than the most necessary implements: some quiet and solitude and a not too incidental hour.

We arrived in Rome about six weeks ago, at a time when it was still the empty, hot, fever-discredited Rome, and this circumstance, together with other practical difficulties in getting settled, helped to make it seem that the unrest around us would not cease and the foreignness lay with the weight of homelessness upon us. Add to this that Rome (if one does not yet know it) has an oppressingly sad effect for the first few days: through the lifeless and doleful museum atmosphere it exhales, through the abundance of its pasts, fetched-forth and laboriously upheld pasts (on which a small present subsists), through the immense overestimation, sustained by savants and philologists and copied by the average traveler in Italy, of all these disfigured and dilapidated things, which at bottom are after all no more than chance remains of another time and of a life that is not and must not be ours. Finally, after weeks of being daily on the defensive, one finds oneself again, if still somewhat confused, and one says to oneself: no, there is not *more* beauty here than elsewhere, and all these objects, continuously admired by generations and patched and mended by workmen's hands, signify nothing, are nothing, and have no heart and no value;—but there is much beauty here, because there is much beauty everywhere. Waters unendingly full of life move along the old aqueducts into the great city and dance in the many squares over white stone basins and spread out in wide spacious pools and murmur by day and lift up their murmuring to the night that is large and starry here and soft with winds. And gardens are here, unforgettable avenues and flights of stairs, stairs devised by Michelangelo, stairs that are built after the pattern of downward-gliding waters—broadly bringing forth step out of step in their descent like wave out of wave. Through such impressions one collects oneself, wins oneself back again out of the pretentious multiplicity that talks and chatters there (and how talkative it is!), and one learns slowly to recognize the very few things in which the eternal endures that one can love and something solitary in which one can quietly take part.

I am still living in the city, on the Capitol, not far from the finest equestrian statue that has come down to us from Roman art—that of Marcus Aurelius; but in a few weeks I shall move into a quiet simple room, an old flat-roofed summerhouse, that lies lost way deep in a large park, hidden from the town, its noise and incident. There I shall live all winter and rejoice in the great quiet, from which I expect the gift of good and industrious hours. . . .

From thence, where I shall be more at home, I will write you a longer letter, further discussing what you have written me. Today I must only tell you (and perhaps it is wrong of me not to have done this before) that the book announced in your letter (which was to contain works of yours) has not arrived here. Has it gone back to you, perhaps from Worpswede? (For one may not forward parcels to foreign countries.) This is the most favorable possibility, and I would like to know it confirmed. I hope there is no question of loss—which, the Italian mails being what they are, would not be anything exceptional—unfortunately.

I would have been glad to get this book (as I would anything that gives a sign of you); and verses that you have written meantime I shall always (if you will confide them to me) read and read again and experience as well and as sincerely as I can. With wishes and greetings,

Yours:
Rainer Maria Rilke

SIX

My dear Mr. Kappus,

You shall not be without a greeting from me when Christmas comes and when you, in the midst of the holiday, are bearing your solitude more heavily than usual. But if then you notice that it is great, rejoice because of this; for what (ask yourself) would solitude be that had no greatness; there is but *one* solitude, and that is great, and not easy to bear, and to almost everybody come hours when they would gladly exchange it for any sort of intercourse, however banal and cheap, for the semblance of some slight accord with the first comer, with the unworthiest. . . . But perhaps those are the very hours when solitude grows; for its growing is painful as the growing of boys and sad as the beginning of springtimes. But that must not mislead you. The necessary thing is after all but this: solitude, great inner solitude. Going-into-oneself and for hours meeting no one—this one must be able to attain. To be solitary, the way one was solitary as a child, when the grownups went around involved with things that seemed important and big because they themselves looked so busy and because one comprehended nothing of their doings.

And when one day one perceives that their occupations are

paltry, their professions petrified and no longer linked with living, why not then continue to look like a child upon it all as upon something unfamiliar, from out of the depth of one's own world, out of the expanse of one's own solitude, which is itself work and status and vocation? Why want to exchange a child's wise incomprehension for defensiveness and disdain, since incomprehension is after all being alone, while defensiveness and disdain are a sharing in that from which one wants by these means to keep apart.

Think, dear sir, of the world you carry within you, and call this thinking what you will; whether it be remembering your own childhood or yearning toward your own future—only be attentive to that which rises up in you and set it above everything that you observe about you. What goes on in your innermost being is worthy of your whole love; you must somehow keep working at it and not lose too much time and too much courage in clarifying your attitude toward people. Who tells you that you have one anyway?— I know, your profession is hard and full of contradiction of yourself, and I foresaw your complaint and knew that it would come. Now that it has come, I cannot comfort you, I can only advise you to consider whether all professions are not like that, full of demands, full of enmity against the individual, saturated as it were with the hatred of those who have found themselves mute and sullen in a humdrum duty. The situation in which you now have to live is no more heavily laden with conventions, prejudices and mistakes than all the other situations, and if there are some that feign a greater freedom, still there is none that is in itself broad and spacious and in contact with the big things of which real living consists. Only the individual who is solitary is like a thing placed under profound laws, and when he goes out into the morning that is just beginning, or looks out into the evening that is full of happening, and if he feels what is going on there, then all status drops from him as from a dead man, though he stands in the midst of sheer life. What you, dear Mr. Kappus, must now experience as an officer, you would have felt just the same in any of the established professions; yes, even if, outside of any position, you had merely sought some light and independent contact with society, this feeling of constraint would not have been spared you.— It is so everywhere; but that is no reason for fear or sorrow; if there is nothing in common between you and other people, try being close to things, they will not desert you; there are the nights still and the winds that go through the trees and across many lands; among things and with the animals everything is still full of happening, in which you may participate; and children are still the way you were as a child, sad like that and happy,—and if you think of your childhood you live among them again, among the solitary children, and the grownups are nothing, and their dignity has no value.

And if it worries and torments you to think of your childhood and of the simplicity and quiet that goes with it, because you cannot believe any more in God, who appears everywhere in it, then ask yourself, dear Mr. Kappus, whether you really have lost God? Is it not rather, that you have never yet possessed him? For when should that have been? Do you believe that a child can hold him, him whom men bear only with effort and whose weight compresses the old? Do you believe that anyone who really has him could lose him like a little stone, or do you not think rather that whoever had him could only be lost by him?— But if you know he was not in your childhood, and not before, if you suspect that Christ was deluded by his longing and Mohammed betrayed by his pride—and if you are terrified to feel that even now he is not, in this hour when we speak of him—what then justifies you in missing him, who never was, like one who has passed away, and in seeking him as though he had been lost?

Why do you not think of him as the coming one, imminent from all eternity, the future one, the final fruit of a tree whose leaves we are? What keeps you from projecting his birth into times that are in process of becoming, and living your life like a painful and beautiful day in the history of a great gestation? For do you not see how everything that happens keeps on being a beginning, and could it not be His beginning, since beginning is in itself always so beautiful? If he is the most perfect, must not the lesser be *before* him, so that he can choose himself out of fullness and overflow?— Must he not be the last, in order to encompass everything within himself, and what meaning would we have if he, whom we long for, had already been?

As the bees bring in the honey, so do we fetch the sweetest out of everything and build Him. With the trivial even, with the insignificant (if it but happens out of love) we make a start, with work and with rest after it, with a silence or with a small solitary joy, with everything that we do alone, without supporters and participants, we begin him whom we shall not live to know, even as our forebears could not live to know us. And yet they, who are long gone, are in us, as predisposition, as burden upon our destiny, as blood that pulsates, and as gesture that rises up out of the depths of time.

Is there anything that can take from you the hope of thus some day being in him, the farthest, the ultimate?

Celebrate Christmas, dear Mr. Kappus, in this devout feeling, that perhaps He needs this very fear of life from you in order to begin; these very days of your transition are perhaps the time when everything in you is working at him, as you have already once, in childhood, breathlessly worked at him. Be patient and without resentment and think that the least we can do is to make his becoming not more difficult for him than the earth makes it for the spring when it wants to come.

And be glad and confident.

Yours:

Rainer Maria Rilke

SEVEN

Rome,
May 14th, 1904

My dear Mr. Kappus,

Much time has gone by since I received your last letter. Do not hold that against me; first it was work, then interruptions and finally a poor state of health that again and again kept me from the answer, which (so I wanted it) was to come to you out of quiet and good days. Now I feel somewhat better again (the opening of spring with its mean, fitful changes was very trying here too) and come to greet you, dear Mr. Kappus, and to tell you (which I do with all my heart) one thing and another in reply to your letter, as well as I know how.

You see—I have copied your sonnet, because I found that it is lovely and simple and born in the form in which it moves with such quiet decorum. It is the best of those of your poems that you have let me read. And now I give you this copy because I know that it is important and full of new experience to come upon a work of one's own again written in a strange hand. Read the lines as though they were someone else's, and you will feel deep within you how much they are your own.

It was a pleasure to me to read this sonnet and your letter often; I thank you for both.

And you should not let yourself be confused in your solitude by the fact that there is something in you that wants to break out of it. This very wish will help you, if you use it quietly, and deliberately and like a tool, to spread out your solitude over wide country. People have (with the help of conventions) oriented all their solutions toward the easy and toward the easiest side of the easy; but it is clear that we must hold to what is difficult; everything alive holds to it, everything in Nature grows and defends itself in its own way and is characteristically and spontaneously itself, seeks at all costs to be so and against all opposition. We know little, but that we must hold to what is difficult is a certainty that will not forsake us; it is good to be solitary, for solitude is difficult; that something is difficult must be a reason the more for us to do it.

To love is good, too: love being difficult. For one human being to love another: that is perhaps the most difficult of all our tasks, the ultimate, the last test and proof, the work for which all other work is but preparation. For this reason young people, who are beginners in everything, cannot yet know love: they have to learn it. With their whole being, with all their forces, gathered close about their lonely, timid, upward-beating heart, they must learn to love. But learning-time is always a long, secluded time, and so loving, for a long while ahead and far on into life, is—solitude, intensified and deepened loneness for him who loves. Love is at first not anything that means merging, giving over, and uniting with another (for what would a union be of something unclarified and unfinished, still subordinate—?), it is a high inducement to the individual to ripen, to become something in himself, to become world, to become world for himself for another's sake, it is a great exacting claim upon him, something that chooses him out and calls him to vast things. Only in this sense, as the task of working at themselves ("to hearken and to hammer day and night"), might young people use the love that is given them. Merging and surrendering and every kind of communion is not for them (who must save and gather for a long, long time still), is the ultimate, is perhaps that for which human lives as yet scarcely suffice.

But young people err so often and so grievously in this: that they (in whose nature it lies to have no patience) fling themselves at each other, when love takes possession of them, scatter themselves, just as they are, in all their untidiness, disorder, confusion. . . . And then what? What is life to do to this heap of half-battered existence which they call their communion and which they would gladly call their happiness, if it were possible, and their future? Thus each loses himself for the sake of the other and loses the other and many others that wanted still to come. And loses the expanses and the possibilities, exchanges the approach and flight of gentle, divining things for an unfruitful perplexity out of which nothing can come any more, nothing save a little disgust, disillusionment and poverty, and rescue in one of the many conventions that have been put up in great number like public refuges along this most dangerous road. No realm of human experience is so well provided with conventions as this: life-preservers of most varied invention, boats and swimming-bladders are here; the social conception has managed to supply shelters of every sort, for, as it was disposed to take love-life as a pleasure, it had also to give it an easy form, cheap, safe and sure, as public pleasures are.

It is true that many young people who love wrongly, that is, simply with abandon and unsolitarily (the average will of course always go on doing so), feel the oppressiveness of a failure and want to make the situation in which they have landed viable and fruitful in their own personal way—; for their nature tells them that, less even than all else that is important, can questions of love be solved publicly and according to this or that agreement; that they are questions, intimate questions from one human being to another, which in any case demand a new, special, *only* personal answer—: but how should they, who have already flung themselves together and no longer mark off and distinguish themselves from each other, who therefore no longer possess anything of their own selves, be able to find a way out of themselves, out of the depth of their already shattered solitude?

They act out of common helplessness, and then, if, with the best intentions, they try to avoid the convention that occurs to them (say, marriage), they land in the tentacles of some less loud, but equally deadly conventional solution; for then everything far around them is—convention; where people act out of a prematurely fused, turbid communion, *every* move is convention: every relation to which such entanglement leads has its convention, be it ever so unusual (that is, in the ordinary sense immoral); why, even separation would here be a conventional step, an impersonal chance decision without strength and without fruit.

Whoever looks seriously at it finds that neither for death, which is difficult, nor for difficult love has any explanation, any solution, any hint or way yet been discerned; and for these two problems that we carry wrapped up and hand on without opening, it will not be possible to discover any general rule resting in agreement. But in the same measure in which we begin as individuals to put life to the test, we shall, being individuals, meet these great things at closer range. The demands which the difficult work of love makes upon our development are more than life-size, and as beginners we are not up to them. But if we nevertheless hold out and take this love upon us as burden and apprenticeship, instead of losing ourselves in all the light and frivolous play, behind which people have hidden from the most earnest earnestness of their existence—then a little progress and an alleviation will perhaps be perceptible to those who come long after us; that would be much.

We are only just now beginning to look upon the relation of one individual person to a second individual objectively and without prejudice, and our attempts to live such associations have no model before them. And yet in the changes brought about by time there is already a good deal that would help our timorous novitiate.

The girl and the woman, in their new, their own unfolding, will but in passing be imitators of masculine ways, good and bad, and repeaters of masculine professions. After the uncertainty of such transitions it will become apparent that women were only going through the profusion and the vicissitude of those (often ridiculous) disguises in order to cleanse their own most characteristic nature of the distorting influences of the other sex. Women, in whom life lingers and dwells more immediately, more fruitfully and more confidently, must surely have become fundamentally riper people, more human people, than easygoing man, who is not pulled down below the surface of life by the weight of any fruit of his body, and who, presumptuous and hasty, undervalues what he thinks he loves. This humanity of woman, borne its full time in suffering and humiliation, will come to light when she will have stripped off the conventions of mere femininity in the mutations of her outward status, and those men who do not yet feel it approaching today will be surprised and struck by it. Some day (and for this, particularly in the northern countries, reliable signs are already speaking and shining), some day there will be girls and women whose name will no longer signify merely an opposite of the masculine, but something in itself, something that makes one think, not of any complement and limit, but only of life and existence: the feminine human being.

This advance will (at first much against the will of the outstripped men) change the love-experience, which is now full of error, will alter it from the ground up, reshape it into a relation that is meant to be of one human being to another, no longer of man to woman. And this more human love (that will fulfill itself, infinitely considerate and gentle, and kind and clear in binding and releasing) will resemble that which we are preparing with struggle and toil, the love that consists in this, that two solitudes protect and border and salute each other.

And this further: do not believe that that great love once enjoined upon you, the boy, was lost; can you say whether great and good desires did not ripen in you at the time, and resolutions by which you are still living today? I believe that that love remains so strong and powerful in your memory because it was your first deep being-alone and the first inward work you did on your life.— All good wishes for you, dear Mr. Kappus!

Yours:
Rainer Maria Rilke

SONETT

Durch mein Leben zittert ohne Klage,
ohne Seufzer ein tiefdunkles Weh.
Meiner Träume reiner Blüthenschnee
ist die Weihe meiner stillsten Tage.

Öfter aber kreuzt die grosse Frage
meinen Pfad. Ich werde klein und geh
kalt vorüber wie an einem See,
dessen Flut ich nicht zu messen wage.

Und dann sinkt ein Leid auf mich, so trübe
wie das Grau glanzarmer Sommernächte,
die ein Stern durchflimmert—dann und wann—:

Meine Hände tasten dann nach Liebe,
weil ich gerne Laute beten möchte,
die mein heisser Mund nicht finden kann. . . .

(Franz Kappus)

SONNET

Through my life there trembles without plaint,
without a sigh a deep-dark melancholy.
The pure and snowy blossoming of my dreams
is the consecration of my stillest days.

But oftentimes the great question crosses
my path. I become small and go
coldly past as though along some lake
whose flood I have not hardihood to measure.

And then a sorrow sinks upon me, dusky
as the gray of lusterless summer nights
through which a star glimmers—now and then—:

My hands then gropingly reach out for love,
because I want so much to pray sounds
that my hot mouth cannot find. . . .

EIGHT

Borgeby gård, Flädie, Sweden,
August 12th, 1904

I want to talk to you again a while, dear Mr. Kappus, although I can say almost nothing that is helpful, hardly anything useful. You have had many and great sadnesses, which passed. And you say that even this passing was hard for you and put you out of sorts. But, please, consider whether these great sadnesses have not rather gone right through the center of yourself? Whether much in you has not altered, whether you have not somewhere, at some point of your being, undergone a change while you were sad? Only those sadnesses are dangerous and bad which one carries about among people in order to drown them out; like sicknesses that are superficially and foolishly treated they simply withdraw and after a little pause break out again the more dreadfully; and accumulate within one and are life, are unlived, spurned, lost life, of which one may die. Were it possible for us to see further than our knowledge reaches, and yet a little way beyond the outworks of our divining, perhaps we would endure our sadnesses with greater confidence than our joys. For they are the moments when something new has entered into us, something unknown; our feelings grow mute in shy perplexity, everything in us withdraws, a stillness comes, and the new, which no one knows, stands in the midst of it and is silent.

I believe that almost all our sadnesses are moments of tension that we find paralyzing because we no longer hear our surprised feelings living. Because we are alone with the alien thing that has entered into our self; because everything intimate and accustomed is for an instant taken away; because we stand in the middle of a transition where we cannot remain standing. For this reason the sadness too passes: the new thing in us, the added thing, has entered into our heart, has gone into its inmost chamber and is not even there any more,—is already in our blood. And we do not learn what it was. We could easily be made to believe that nothing has happened, and yet we have changed, as a house changes into which a guest has entered. We cannot say who has come, perhaps we shall never know, but many signs indicate that the future enters into us in this way in order to transform itself in us long before it happens. And this is why it is so important to be lonely and attentive when one is sad: because the apparently uneventful and stark moment at which our future sets foot in us is so much closer to life than that other noisy and fortuitous point of time at which it happens to us as if from outside. The more still, more patient and more open we are when we are sad, so much the deeper and so much the more unswervingly does the new go into us, so much the better do we make it ours, so much the more will it be *our* destiny, and when on some later day it "happens" (that is, steps forth out of us to others), we shall feel in our inmost selves akin and near to it. And that is necessary. It is necessary—and toward this our development will move gradually—that nothing strange should befall us, but only that which has long belonged to us. We have already had to rethink so many of our concepts of motion, we will also gradually learn to realize that that which we call destiny goes forth from within people, not from without into them. Only because so many have not absorbed their destinies and transmuted them within themselves while they were living in them, have they not recognized what has gone forth out of them; it was so strange to them that, in their bewildered fright, they thought it must only just then have entered into them, for they swear never before to have found anything like it in themselves. As people were long mistaken about the motion of the sun, so they are even yet mistaken about the motion of that which is to come. The future stands firm, dear Mr. Kappus, but we move in infinite space.

How should it not be difficult for us?

And to speak of solitude again, it becomes always clearer that this is at bottom not something that one can take or leave. We *are* solitary. We may delude ourselves and act as though this were not so. That is all. But how much better it is to realize that we are so, yes, even to begin by assuming it. We shall indeed turn dizzy then; for all points upon which our eye has been accustomed to rest are taken from us, there is nothing near any more and everything far is infinitely far. A person removed from his own room, almost without preparation and transition, and set upon the height of a great mountain range, would feel something of the sort: an unparalleled insecurity, an abandonment to something inexpressible would almost annihilate him. He would think himself falling or hurled out into space, or exploded into a thousand pieces: what a monstrous lie his brain would have to invent to catch up with and explain the state of his senses! So for him who becomes solitary all distances, all measures change; of these changes many take place suddenly, and then, as with the man on the mountaintop, extraordinary imaginings and singular sensations arise that seem to grow out beyond all bearing. But it is necessary for us to experience *that* too. We must assume our existence as *broadly* as we in any way can; everything, even the unheard-of, must be possible in it. That is at bottom the only courage that is demanded of us: to have courage for the most strange, the most singular and the most inexplicable that we may encounter. That mankind has in this sense been cowardly has done life endless harm; the experiences that are called "visions," the whole so-called "spirit-world," death, all those things that are so closely akin to us, have by daily parrying been so crowded out of life that the senses with which we could have grasped them are atrophied. To say nothing of God. But fear of the inexplicable has not alone impoverished the existence of the individual; the relationship between one human being and another has also been cramped by it, as though it had been lifted out of the riverbed of endless possibilities and set down in a fallow spot on the bank, to which nothing happens. For it is not inertia alone that is responsible for human relationships repeating themselves from case to case, indescribably monotonous and unrenewed; it is shyness before any sort of new, unforeseeable experience with which one does not think oneself able to cope. But only someone who is ready for everything, who excludes nothing, not even the most enigmatical, will live the relation to another as something alive and will himself draw exhaustively from his own existence. For if we think of this existence of the individual as a larger or smaller room, it appears evident that most people learn to know only a corner of their room, a place by the window, a strip of floor on which they walk up and down. Thus they have a certain security. And yet that dangerous insecurity is so much more human which drives the prisoners in Poe's stories to feel out the shapes of their horrible dungeons and not be strangers to the unspeakable terror of their abode. We, however, are not prisoners. No traps or snares are set about us, and there is nothing which should intimidate or worry us. We are set down in life as in the element to which we best correspond, and over and above this we have through thousands of years of accommodation become so like this life, that when we hold still we are, through a happy mimicry, scarcely to be distinguished from all that surrounds us. We have no reason to mistrust our world, for it is not against us. Has it terrors, they are *our* terrors; has it abysses, those abysses belong to us; are dangers at hand, we must try to love them. And if only we arrange our life according to that principle which counsels us that we must always hold to the difficult, then that which now still seems to us the most alien will become what we most trust and find most faithful. How should we be able to forget those ancient myths that are at the beginning of all peoples, the myths about dragons that at the last moment turn into princesses; perhaps all the dragons of our lives are princesses who are only waiting to see us once beautiful and brave. Perhaps everything terrible is in its deepest being something helpless that wants help from us.

So you must not be frightened, dear Mr. Kappus, if a sadness rises up before you larger than any you have ever seen; if a restiveness, like light and cloud-shadows, passes over your hands and over all you do. You must think that something is happening with you, that life has not forgotten you, that it holds you in its hand; it will not let you fall. Why do you want to shut out of your life any agitation, any pain, any melancholy, since you really do not know what these states are working upon you? Why do you want to persecute yourself with the question whence all this may be coming and whither it is bound? Since you know that you are in the midst of transitions and wished for nothing so much as to change. If there is anything morbid in your processes, just remember that sickness is the means by which an organism frees itself of foreign matter; so one must just help it to be sick, to have its whole sickness and break out with it, for that is its progress. In you, dear Mr. Kappus, so much is now happening; you must be patient as a sick man and confident as a convalescent; for perhaps you are both. And more: you are the doctor too, who has to watch over himself. But there are in every illness many days when the doctor can do nothing but wait. And this it is that you, insofar as you are your own doctor, must now above all do.

Do not observe yourself too much. Do not draw too hasty conclusions from what happens to you; let it simply happen to you. Otherwise you will too easily look with reproach (that is, morally) upon your past, which naturally has its share in all that you are now meeting. But that part of the errors, desires and longings of your boyhood which is working in you is not what you remember and condemn. The unusual conditions of a lonely and helpless childhood are so difficult, so complicated, open to so many influences and at the same time so disengaged from all real connections with life that, where a vice enters into it, one may not without more ado simply call it vice. One must be so careful with names anyway; it is so often on the *name* of a misdeed that a life goes to pieces, not the nameless and personal action itself, which was perhaps a perfectly definite necessity of that life and would have been absorbed by it without effort. And the expenditure of energy seems to you so great only because you overvalue victory; it is not the victory that is the "great thing" you think to have done, although you are right in your feeling; the great thing is that there was already something there which you could put in the place of that delusion, something true and real. Without this even your victory would have been but a moral reaction, without wide significance, but thus it has become a segment of your life. Your life, dear Mr. Kappus, of which I think with so many wishes. Do you remember how that life yearned out of its childhood for the "great"? I see that it is now going on beyond the great to long for greater. For this reason it will not cease to be difficult, but for this reason too it will not cease to grow.

And if there is one thing more that I must say to you, it is this: Do not believe that he who seeks to comfort you lives untroubled among the simple and quiet words that sometimes do you good. His life has much difficulty and sadness and remains far behind yours. Were it otherwise he would never have been able to find those words.

Yours:
Rainer Maria Rilke

NINE

My dear Mr. Kappus,

in this time that has gone by without a letter I have been partly traveling, partly so busy that I could not write. And even today writing comes hard to me because I have already had to write a lot of letters so that my hand is tired. If I could dictate, I would say a great deal to you, but as it is, take only a few words for your long letter.

I think of you, dear Mr. Kappus, often and with such concentrated wishes that that really ought to help you somehow. Whether my letters can really be a help, I often doubt. Do not say: yes, they are. Just accept them and without much thanks, and let us await what comes.

There is perhaps no use my going into your particular points now; for what I could say about your tendency to doubt or about your inability to bring outer and inner life into unison, or about all the other things that worry you—: it is always what I have already said: always the wish that you may find patience enough in yourself to endure, and simplicity enough to believe; that you may acquire more and more confidence in that which is difficult, and in your solitude among others. And for the rest, let life happen to you. Believe me: life is right, in any case.

And about emotions: all emotions are pure which gather you and lift you up; that emotion is impure which seizes only *one* side of your being and so distorts you. Everything that you can think in the face of your childhood, is right. Everything that makes *more* of you than you have heretofore been in your best hours, is right. Every heightening is good if it is in your *whole* blood, if it is not intoxication, not turbidity, but joy which one can see clear to the bottom. Do you understand what I mean?

And your doubt may become a good quality if you *train it*. It must become *knowing*, it must become critical. Ask it, whenever it wants to spoil something for you, *why* something is ugly, demand proofs from it, test it, and you will find it perplexed and embarrassed perhaps, or perhaps rebellious. But don't give in, insist on arguments and act this way, watchful and consistent, every single time, and the day will arrive when from a destroyer it will become one of your best workers—perhaps the cleverest of all that are building at your life.

That is all, dear Mr. Kappus, that I am able to tell you today. But I am sending you at the same time the reprint of a little poetical work* that has now appeared in the Prague periodical *Deutsche Arbeit*. There I speak to you further of life and of death and of how both are great and splendid.

Yours:
Rainer Maria Rilke

* The Lay of the Love and Death of Cornet Otto [*subsequent editions*: Christoph] Rilke, *familiarly and very widely known as "the* Cornet," *had been written in* 1899.

TEN

the day after Christmas, 1908

You must know, dear Mr. Kappus, how glad I was to have that lovely letter from you. The news you give me, real and tellable as it now is again, seems good to me, and, the longer I have thought it over, the more I have felt it to be in fact good. I really wanted to write you this for Christmas Eve; but what with work, in which I am living this winter, variously and uninterruptedly, the ancient holiday approached so fast that I had hardly any time left to attend to the most necessary errands, much less to write.

But I have thought of you often during these holidays and imagined how quiet you must be in your lonely fort among the empty hills, upon which those big southerly winds precipitate themselves as though they would devour them in great pieces.

The stillness must be immense in which such sounds and movements have room, and when one thinks that to it all the presence of the far-off sea comes chiming in as well, perhaps as the inmost tone in that prehistoric harmony, then one can only wish for you that you are confidently and patiently letting that lofty solitude work upon you which is no more to be stricken out of your life; which in everything there is ahead of you to experience and to do will work as an anonymous influence, continuously and gently decisive, much as in us blood of ancestors ceaselessly stirs and mingles with our own into that unique, not repeatable being which at every turning of our life we are.

Yes: I am glad you have that steady expressible existence with you, that title, that uniform, that service, all that tangible and limited reality, which in such surroundings, with a similarly isolated and not numerous command, takes on seriousness and necessity, implies a vigilant application above and beyond the military profession's tendency to play and to pass the time, and not only allows but actually cultivates a self-reliant attentiveness. And to be among conditions that work at us, that set us before big natural things from time to time, is all we need.

Art too is only a way of living, and, however one lives, one can, unwittingly, prepare oneself for it; in all that is real one is closer to it and more nearly neighbored than in the unreal half-artistic professions, which, while they pretend proximity to some art, in practice belie and assail the existence of all art, as for instance the whole of journalism does and almost all criticism and three-quarters of what is called and wants to be called literature. I am glad, in a word, that you have surmounted the danger of falling into this sort of thing and are somewhere in a rough reality being solitary and courageous. May the year that is at hand uphold and strengthen you in that.

Ever yours:
Rainer Maria Rilke

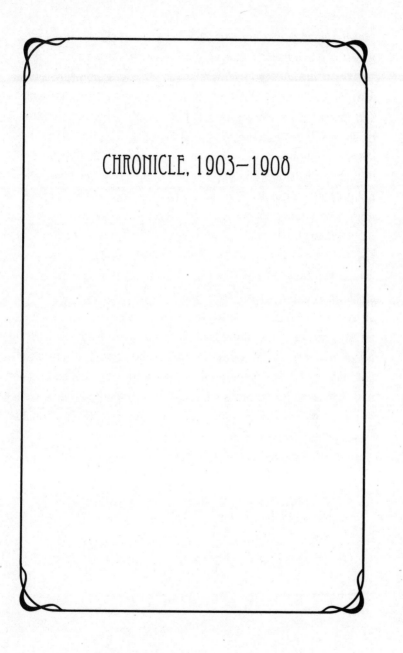

CHRONICLE, 1903–1908